Drawing Sharks, Whales, Dolphins, and Seals

Drawing Sharks, Whales, Dolphins, and Seals

by Paul Frame

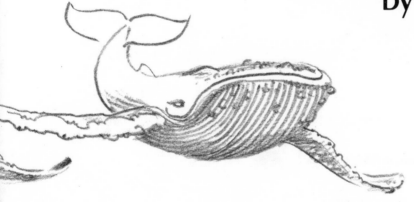

A How-to-Draw Book

FRANKLIN WATTS
New York / London / Toronto / Sydney
1983

to Judie Mills and Frank Sloan
Judie—for making the physical appearance of this book
    so clean and open
Frank—for making my text so understandable

Library of Congress Cataloging in Publication Data

Frame, Paul, 1913-
Drawing sharks, whales, dolphins, and seals.

(A How-to-draw book)
Summary: Explains general drawing techniques and tools
and gives specific instructions for drawing sea mammals.
1. Sharks in art—Juvenile literature. 2. Marine
mammals in art—Juvenile literature. 3. Drawing—Technique—Juvenile literature. [1. Marine mammals in art.
2. Drawing—Technique] I. Title. II. Series.
NC781.F7 1983   743'.695   82-23737
ISBN 0-531-04541-2

CONTENTS

INTRODUCTION

Whenever the subject of drawing arises,
one of the most frequent statements you hear is
"Oh, I can't draw. I can't even draw a straight
line with a ruler."

Not true.

First, you *can* draw. If you can write
well enough for someone else to read your writing,
you can draw. The only question is how well. That,
to no small degree, will depend upon how much you
want to draw.

The next thing to remember in drawing
is that you'll never need (nor should you ever
use) a ruler unless you are doing an architectural
rendering.

The only other ingredients you will need
are concentration and practice. Follow the
few simple rules mentioned in this book, add generous
amounts of the above-mentioned ingredients, and in
a few weeks you will both surprise and please
yourself.

Try it! You'll see.

CHAPTER 1
First Things First

You will need the following supplies to
start. Later on, as your skills grow, you will want
to experiment with other materials. For the
time being, start with these basics:

Drawing board: Any rigid,
smooth surface about 14 to 18
inches (36 to 46 cm) wide and
20 to 24 inches (51 to 61 cm)
long. To make a simple drawing
surface, use ¼-inch (0.64-cm)
plywood or glue together three pieces of
thick industrial cardboard or
corrugated board. Take care to alternate
the ribbing as shown.

Paper: Paper is expensive and you'll use
a lot of it. For practice sessions, use large grocery
bags. Slit these down one side and at the bottom.
If they are very wrinkled, dampen them slightly.
Then press them dry with a steam iron.

Old newspapers are useful. Buy a can of liquid gesso from a paint or art supply store. Apply two coats of the gesso to each side of each sheet, allowing fifteen minutes drying time between coats. This will not cover the print completely, but it will take care of an area large enough for your practice sessions.

One quart (.95 l) should cover 250 sheets. If you are feeling rich, buy a 19- by 24-inch (48- by 61-cm) newsprint pad. This is good for practice sessions. For your more finished efforts, there are all kinds of sketch pads at your local art, variety, or stationery store. Experiment until you find the surface you like best.

Tools: Pencils top the list; soft leads such as HB or 2B are best. During damp or humid weather you may find that 4B or 6B work even better.

You have a wide choice of kinds of pencils. There are the usual wood-cased pencils; you won't have to sharpen the slender leads (HB or 2B) frequently except when you need fine detail.

There are also a number of inexpensive automatic pencils (A).

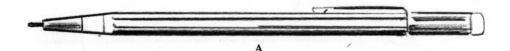

A

Lead holders (B) are another choice.
Leads for these holders range from 8H (very
hard) to 6B (very soft). These leads are
usually somewhat thicker than those used in
automatic pencils. For this reason you may
find a sandpaper block (C) useful for sharpening.

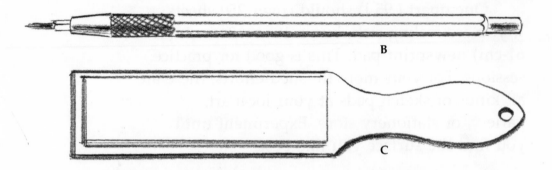

You can save money by making your own
sandpaper block. Buy several sheets of 00 sandpaper
and cut into 1- by 4-inch (2.5- by 10-cm) strips.
Then staple six or eight strips to a heavy piece
of cardboard (D).

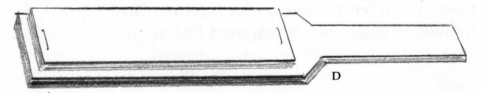

Pencil Holders: It is wasteful not to use pencil
stubs. So a pencil holder (E) is a good tool to
add.

Large Clip: A large paper clip like the one shown
(F) is very useful for holding loose drawing papers or
your pad to your drawing board. These clips
can usually be found in a stationery or variety
store.

F

Erasers: The most useful kind is a kneaded
eraser (G). It can be squeezed into many
shapes and sizes and does less to disturb the
surface of your paper.

G

A kneaded eraser is also very effective for
lightening a line or an area of shading without totally
erasing it. To do this, *do not* rub as you would with
other erasers. Place the eraser on the area or line
to be lightened, *press down*, then lift up. Repeat
until you have the tonal value you want.

Another type of eraser is art gum. This is the
best kind to use on a delicate or glossy surfaced
paper.

Fixative: You will need this if you want to keep your pencil sketch from smudging. Ask for a workable, matte finish fixative.

Tracing Paper: It comes in three different-size pads: 9 by 12 inches (23 by 30 cm), 14 by 17 inches (36 by 43 cm), and 19 by 24 inches (48 by 61 cm). You will find this to be invaluable over the next few months. Suggestions for its use will come later on.

Sketch Book: Pick one that fits in your pocket. Get in the habit of carrying it with you at all times. There's nothing like sketching to increase your skill. It's like taking notes so you'll learn to see and remember what you have looked at.

If sharks or whales are your main interest, you'll find that developing the habit of making quick sketches of anything that catches your eye will pay off.

Instead of a pencil, carry a ballpoint pen. These pens don't smudge, and they tend to make you do simpler sketches.

Reference File: A file of photographs of any and all things that interest you will be an excellent source of information if you are at all serious about your drawing. Ask your local librarian for a list of suggested publications that cover the areas of your special interest.

Then ask among your friends to see if they subscribe to any of the publications on the list. Clip from newspapers and old catalogs. Divide the clippings by subjects: whales, sharks, dolphins, etc. Put each one in a separate folder.

You can save money by making your own folders. Use cardboard or corrugated board. See A.

Cut pieces that measure 17 by 10 inches (43 by 25 cm). Fold 8 inches (20 cm) on each side, leaving 1 inch (2.5 cm) in the middle. Label the outside to show what each folder contains.

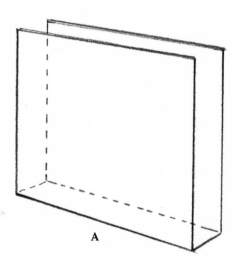

A

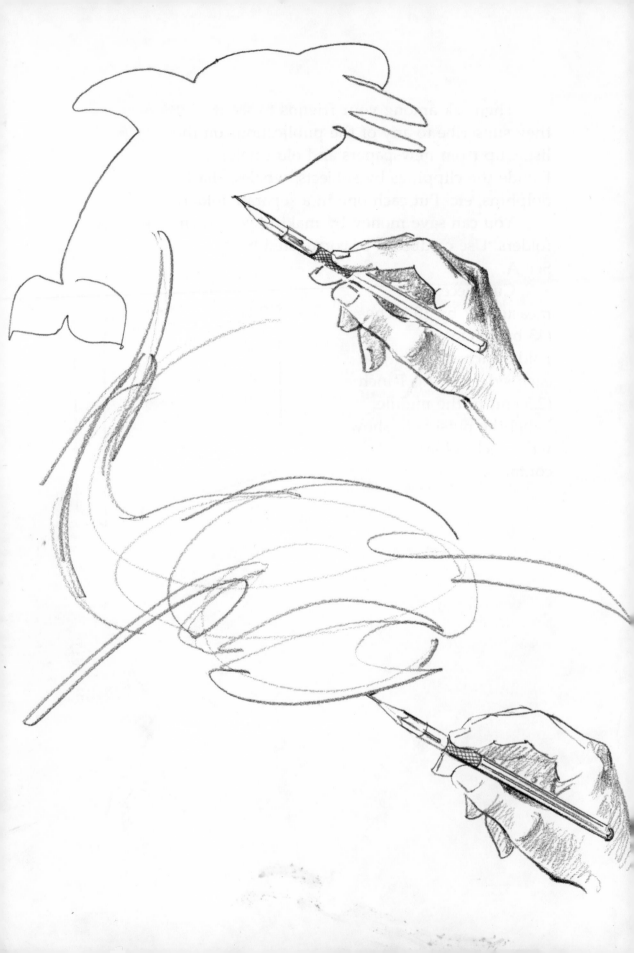

CHAPTER 2
Exercises

There are three parts of you that must work almost as one when you sketch. Your eyes, your brain, and your hand must learn to work as a team.

Until you become very skilled, the following two exercises are an extremely good way to get all your "juices" going. Try each exercise for about ten minutes before you start sketching.

Contour Drawing: Use scrap paper and a 2B or 4B pencil or lead. Seat yourself in a relaxed, comfortable position 6 to 8 feet (1.8 to 2.4 m) from a very simple subject. Pick a starting point along the contour of the object. Now place your pencil on the paper and try to imagine that the pencil is actually touching the contour. *Do not take your eyes away from the object to look at your paper.*

Think of your eyes and the pencil as *one* and move them slowly along the contour.

You'll be tempted to look at your paper; don't. Move very deliberately and try to feel as if you are actually tracing the form.

Raise your pencil only when you feel you've reached your starting point. If there are details within the subject, pick a new starting point and repeat the procedure.

Your first efforts will look very distorted, but don't be upset. No one ever learned a difficult task right away.

As with all your work, keep dated examples of each session; after about a month, look them over. You will be both surprised and pleased.

Gesture Drawing: In this exercise your main effort should be to dramatize *what* your subject is doing. Don't make a conscious effort to draw correctly.

Try very hard to capture the mood and/or the action without worrying about proper proportions. Spend about two minutes on each sketch.

Do not lift your pencil from the paper. Sketch with long, sweeping strokes, using your whole arm rather than your fingers and wrist.

You'll need rather large scrap paper for this. Save and date sketches from each session. This record gives you a very instructive look at your progress.

17

CHAPTER 3
Anatomy

To understand fully what you are drawing, you should look at the subjects
from the bones out.

Drawing sharks, whales, dolphins, and
seals is a different task from drawing people
or land animals. The skeletons seldom
have as direct an influence on their silhouettes
as with people or animals. This means that
you must observe the few reference points
very carefully.

There is one feature you will notice
that all these creatures have in common.
Unlike most other inhabitants of this planet,
their shapes let the creatures function superbly
in their natural habitat: water.

One other important note. In each
case you should strive for a look of *bulk*
and *roundness*. Light and shade, which will be
discussed in the next chapter, will help you
achieve this.

19

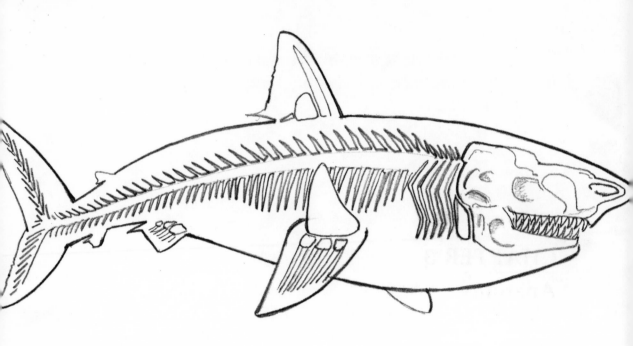

The great white shark: This is the shark
with the most fearsome reputation. For
the most part the only skeletal differences
among various types of sharks will be found
in the skull. On page 22 you will see some
of the more interesting types.

Of the subjects covered in this book,
the shark is the only one that evolved in
the sea and has remained there.

Science knows of 250 kinds of sharks.
Of this number ten are known to eat
humans. They are the great white, gray,
tiger, hammerhead, lemon, whitetip,
mako, sand, nurse, and blue.

Their greatest differences from sea mammals
are their gills (organs for getting oxygen from
water) and how their tails are set on their
bodies.

This is important to you as it makes their swimming motion quite different. The shark's tail is attached to its body in a vertical fashion as shown in A. This makes it necessary to use a side-to-side motion (B), as all members of the fish family do.

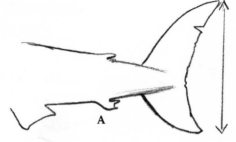

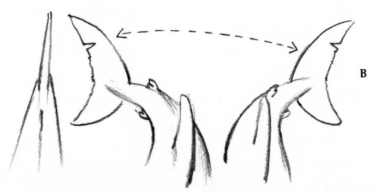

Whales and their cousins the dolphins are just the opposite. Their flukes (tails) are horizontal (C) and therefore used in an up-and-down motion (D). They use the last quarter of their bodies to propel themselves through water.

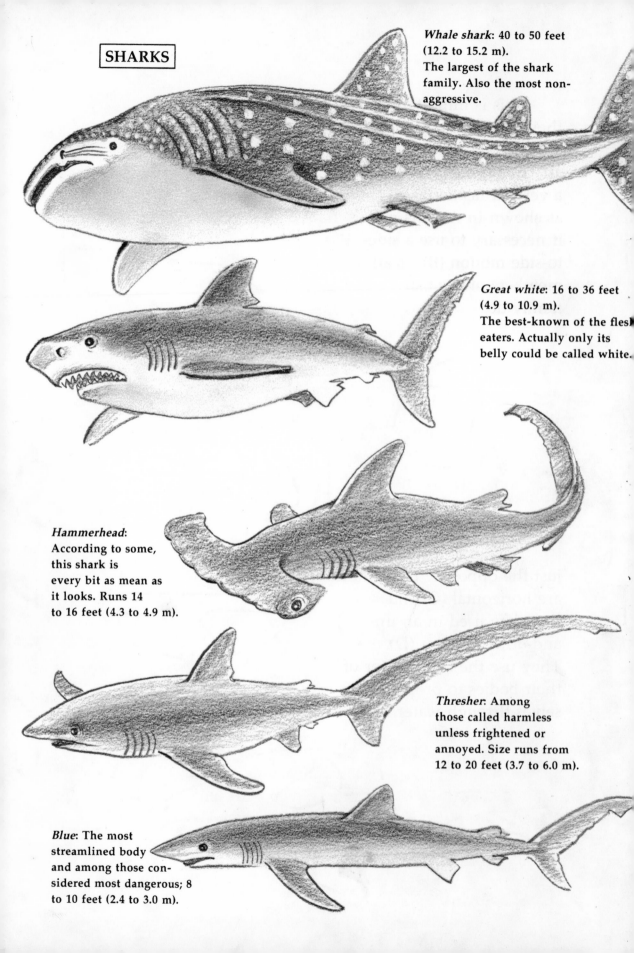

SHARKS

Whale shark: 40 to 50 feet (12.2 to 15.2 m). The largest of the shark family. Also the most non-aggressive.

Great white: 16 to 36 feet (4.9 to 10.9 m). The best-known of the flesh eaters. Actually only its belly could be called white.

Hammerhead: According to some, this shark is every bit as mean as it looks. Runs 14 to 16 feet (4.3 to 4.9 m).

Thresher: Among those called harmless unless frightened or annoyed. Size runs from 12 to 20 feet (3.7 to 6.0 m).

Blue: The most streamlined body and among those considered most dangerous; 8 to 10 feet (2.4 to 3.0 m).

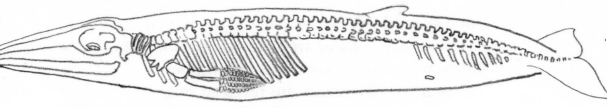

Blue Whale: At 90 or more feet (27.4 m), the blue whale is the largest of the whales. Because it has been hunted almost to extinction, it is now protected. While nursing its young, a blue can gain as much as 200 pounds (91 kg) a day! A mature blue can eat eight tons of food a day.

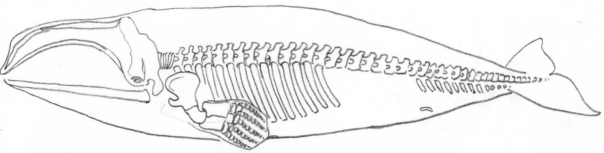

Right whale: Along with the bowhead, the right whales are the slowest moving of the whale family. This may be in part because these three share a more blunt, less streamlined kind of silhouette.

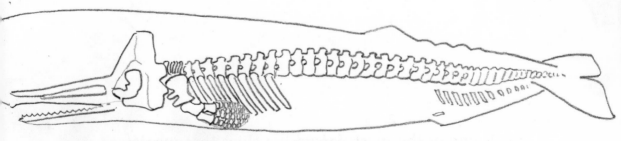

Sperm whale: Perhaps the most famous and most numerous of the whale family. The sperm whale provides the substance so valuable to makers of perfume: ambergris.

The three skeletal profiles on page 23 show you that, anatomically, whales are remarkably alike. The real differences are in their skulls and flippers.

The greatest differences are revealed in the skulls, as you can see on page 23. The surface difference in the flippers from species to species is not great except in the humpback. Theirs are oversized. Note also the similarity to a human arm and hand.

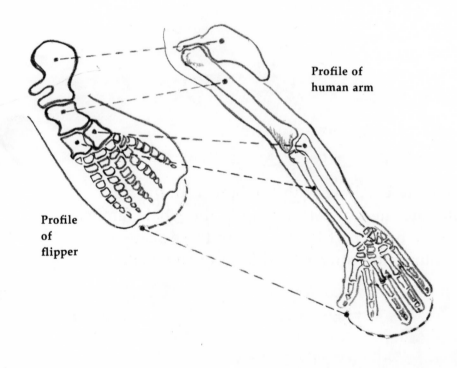

Profile of human arm

Profile of flipper

This is one of the most persuasive clues that whales, dolphins, and seals returned to the sea fifty million years ago, having been land mammals at one time.

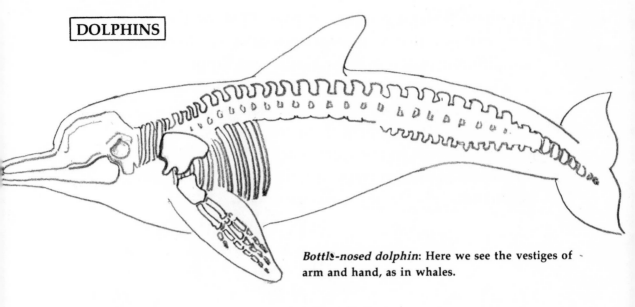

DOLPHINS

Bottle-nosed dolphin: Here we see the vestiges of arm and hand, as in whales.

The dolphin is really a member of one group of whales called the toothed. The other group consists of baleen whales. The two groups have about one hundred species, almost half of which are dolphins. The most widely recognized and most appealing (to humans) is the bottle-nosed. It is the bottle-nosed we will be concerned with.

When studying this profile view, you should look especially at two characteristics. Notice how streamlined the dolphin is. You see no really blunt edges, only soft and molded curves. Notice the area where the backbone thickens, heavy with muscle tissue. It is the "power pack," which moves dolphins through the water at a speed of 30 knots (30 nautical miles, or 56 km) per hour.

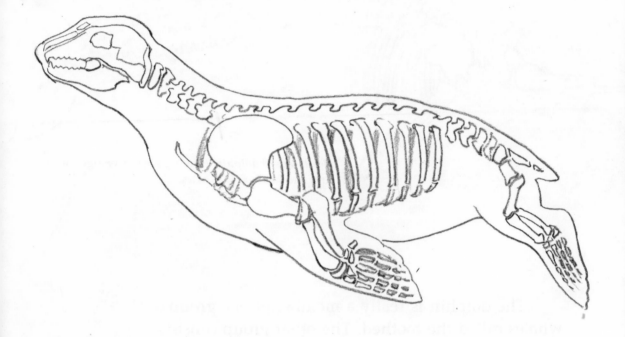

Seals are classified into three groups. Within those three groups there are about thirty species.

The three groups are (1) eared seals and sea lions, (2) the true seals and sea elephants, and (3) walruses.

The species you are probably most familiar with is the sea lion. Sea lions perform in circuses and are most frequently seen in zoos.

Examples of each group will be shown, with emphasis on the sea lion.

Sea lion: Smallish member of the three groups and a graceful swimmer. When you draw them in the water, remember to concentrate on a sleek ballet-like grace. Also be aware that they use their front flippers much more as an actual swimming aid than others with this equipment do.

Sea elephant: This is the largest of the true seal group, 16 feet (4.9 m) long, 12 feet (3.7 m) wide, and the trunk 15 inches (38 cm). Fully grown, a bull sea elephant weighs about 5,000 pounds (2,268 kg). Whalers have slaughtered them heavily, but at least 300,000 may be found in Antarctica and on Guadalupe Island, off Lower California.

Walrus: 1½ tons of placid, caring
parent. They have never been known to
attack humans *unless* their young are
threatened; then they are fierce indeed.
They are now found mostly in the Bering
Sea, where they use their great tusks to
dig up shellfish from the bottom.

When sketching the walrus or the sea
elephant (and to a lesser degree, the
seal or sea lion), you must observe the
reference material very closely.
Look carefully at what you see; you must try to
give every form a meaning.

CHAPTER 4
Light and Shade

So far we have been talking mostly about
the *form* of sharks, whales, dolphins, and seals.
Your rough sketches have shown the outline and
general appearance of these creatures.

To do complete justice to any of the subjects in this book, you must add touches that will
give each of them a look of weight and very solid
roundness. It is not always easy to endow a simple
drawing with these qualities.

Look at the drawings on pages 22, 27, and 28.
In all these drawings, tone has been added to
give a sense of light and shade.

Look at the cylinder (A) and the ball (B)
below. Look at the light source and see how it
gives these objects areas of light and shade.

Light   Source

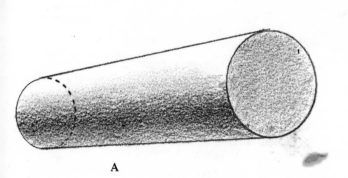

A

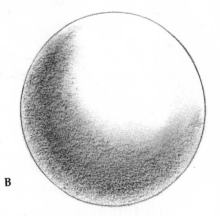

B

In the drawings below you see a simplified formula for giving a form a look of roundness and weight. There are only three tonal values used.

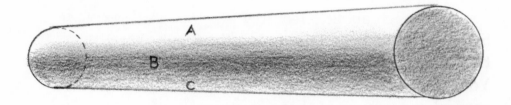

A. Direct light, lightest in tonal value.
B. The area most removed from any light source and therefore having the darkest tonal value.
C. Reflected light, a tonal value lighter than B and darker than A.

Bull shark

When you start drawing more complex forms, this formula may be too simplified. For the most part, however, you will be able to use it.

It might be wise at this point to have at hand both a cylinder and a ball. The ball you can get easily; make the cylinder from any fairly heavy white paper.

Hold each about 3 feet (0.9 m) from a bright light source. Change the angle of the light source and watch how the shadows change with each angle change.

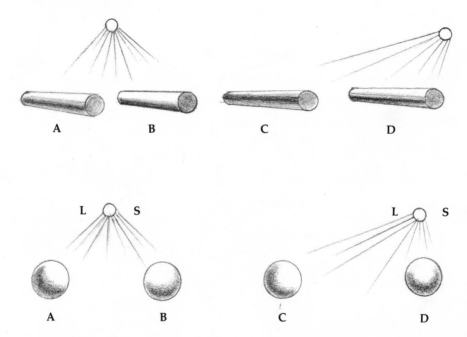

A few words here about reflected light. Light always reaches beyond your object and usually strikes another surface (E). This second surface will then reflect the light and throw a diminished light back to your object.

E. Second, and reflecting, surface

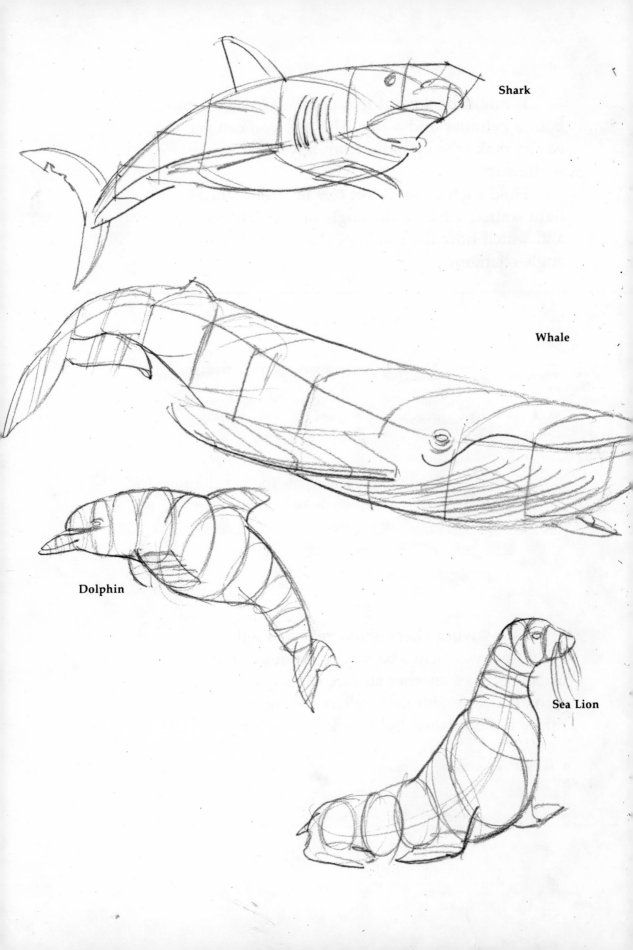

Shark

Whale

Dolphin

Sea Lion

CHAPTER 5
Let's Draw!

It is time to put all the elements together
the result should be a sketch!

Don't expect too much of your first efforts
unless you've been drawing for some time before
you read this book. Unless you are a true genius,
whatever skill you have can only grow if you
practice.

The drawings and information in this chapter
will give you material to use as reference. Don't
just copy what you see on the surface. Instead,
think through to the *unseen* side. In that way you
will give more life and substance to your work.
Remember that your sketches are lines that are
enclosing a form; they are not just an outline.

Don't lose heart. The greatest artists have not
always had an easy time of it. You must look to
your growth.

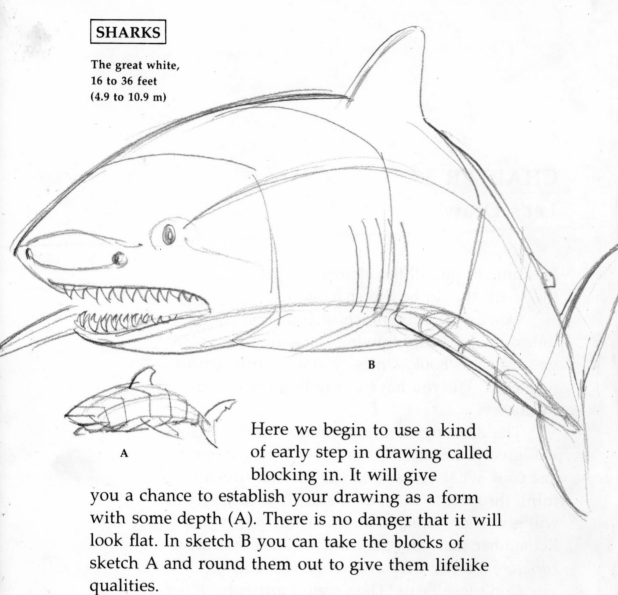

SHARKS

The great white,
16 to 36 feet
(4.9 to 10.9 m)

B

A

Here we begin to use a kind of early step in drawing called blocking in. It will give you a chance to establish your drawing as a form with some depth (A). There is no danger that it will look flat. In sketch B you can take the blocks of sketch A and round them out to give them lifelike qualities.

All of this early blocking in should be done on tracing paper. Make a basic sketch as in A. Then do your refining as in B directly on top of the first sketch by folding your tracing paper over. In this way you will be able to keep a visual record of your progress. Use this method until you can sketch and "feel" the unseen side.

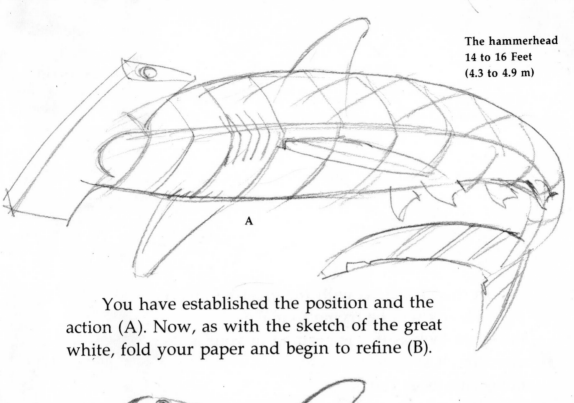

A

You have established the position and the action (A). Now, as with the sketch of the great white, fold your paper and begin to refine (B).

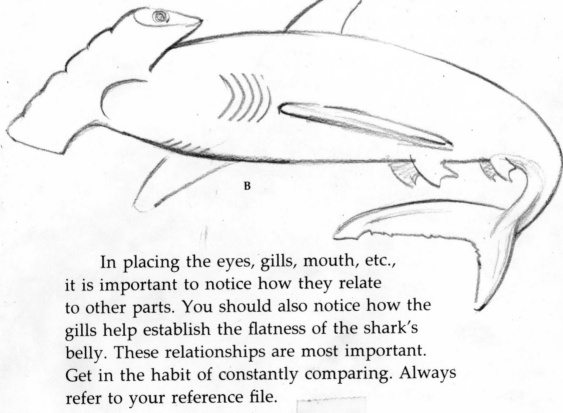

B

In placing the eyes, gills, mouth, etc., it is important to notice how they relate to other parts. You should also notice how the gills help establish the flatness of the shark's belly. These relationships are most important. Get in the habit of constantly comparing. Always refer to your reference file.

35

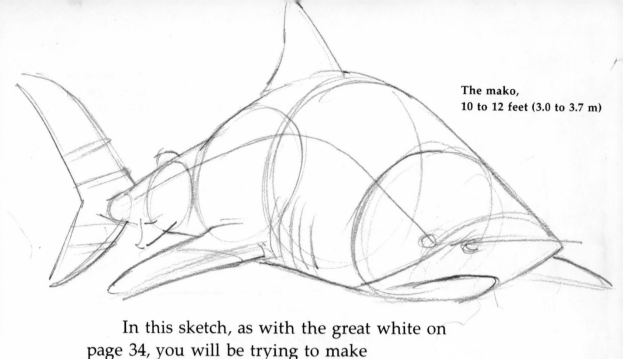

In this sketch, as with the great white on page 34, you will be trying to make the shark look as if it is heading in your direction. It is important to set the shark at an angle that stresses its head, the closest part to you.

Tone has been added. This gives the sketch a more finished look.

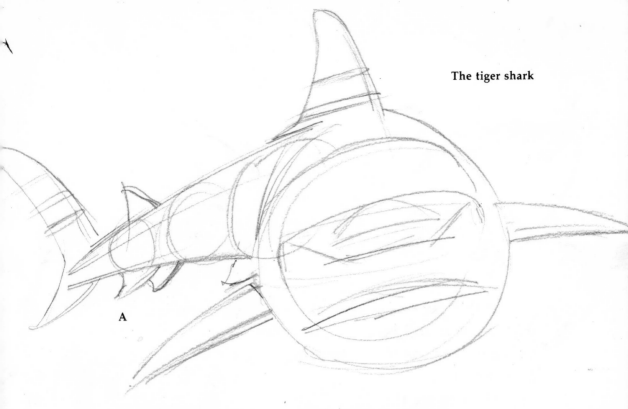

A

Here's an even more frontal view in which
you sketch the body, up to the pectoral fin, head on.
From the fin the back is seen in profile, almost at
a right angle. Here also B has been given more
finished treatment.

B

Whitetip

By now you know how to block in and add details such as eyes, mouth, gill, etc. The only step shown in this drawing is the one where tone has been added to provide roundness and sharpened details.

The common thresher,
12 to 20 feet
(3.7 to 6.0 m)

This is a very "drawable" shark, principally
because of the streamerlike tail assembly.

Use this sketch as reference and begin to
add some underwater environment. It would be a
good idea to collect as many photographs of
underwater scenes as you can find for your file.
Try to keep the use of tone as simple as possible.

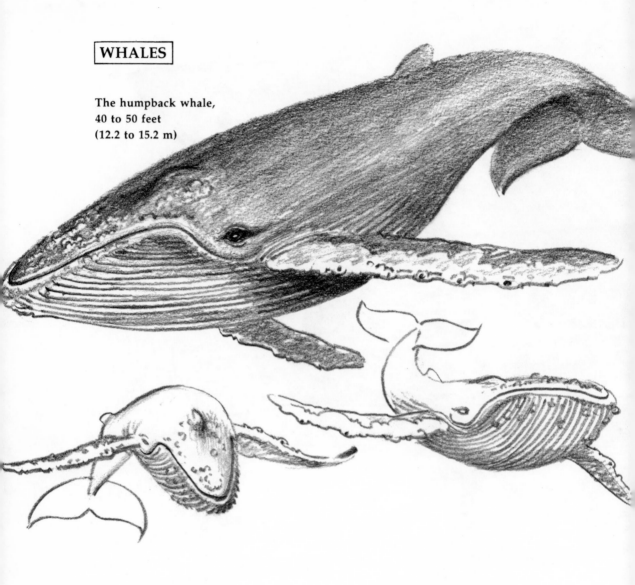

WHALES

The humpback whale,
40 to 50 feet
(12.2 to 15.2 m)

The humpback, the singer of songs, is the whale
that at least one expert feels has a sense of humor.
The humpback is most likely to breach (leap almost
clear of the water), heaving all 30 to 40 tons of
its great body with only the power of its flukes
(tail). The smaller sketches show how gracefully
this whale swims in spite of its size.

Try sketching this scene,
keeping to simple
tonal areas.

Here is a humpback whale breaching—a truly
awesome sight! See how the humpback arches
over, with a belly-up movement—a thrilling
spectacle. No one knows why they breach. Some
theories say it is to dislodge a parasite; others that
it is part of a ritual greeting.

41

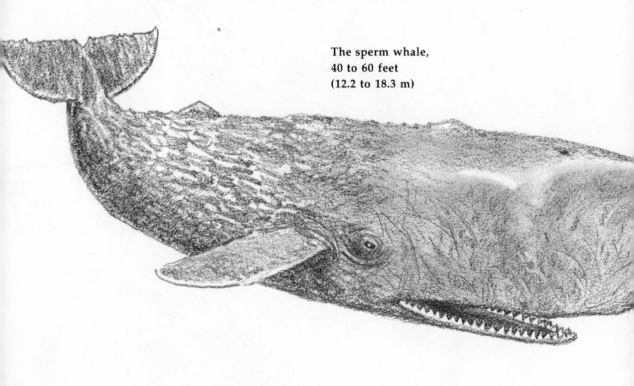

The sperm whale,
40 to 60 feet
(12.2 to 18.3 m)

This is the same kind of whale as the famous Moby Dick. As far as we know, there are more sperm whales than any other of the great whales.

The numerous scars you see around the nose and mouth are the result of its favorite food, squid. It is the squid's beak that causes our friend's nose area to look like a battleground.

With this great mammal your challenge will be to keep your sketch from looking like a big boxcar with wings. The most difficult area will be aft of the flippers, where you will need to create a sense of motion.

The blue whale,
90 to 100 feet
(27.4 to 30.5 m)

There is doubt among Greenpeace and other conservation groups that there are enough of these, the largest mammals ever on this planet, to insure their survival.

Their young, while feeding, may gain as much as 200 pounds (90 kg) a day. When fully grown, they will devour as much as 8 tons of plankton a day.

The drawing above was sketched and transferred onto watercolor paper. Then a wash was laid on. See the next chapter for details on how you can achieve this result.

The right whale,
50 to 58 feet
(15.2 m to 17.7 m)

The right whale got its name from the early
hunters because it is a slow swimmer. It also floats
when dead and contains large quantities of oil
and baleen (whalebone). It thus became known
as the "right" whale.

The right whale also conveniently keeps to
coastal waters. All of these traits together have
placed it on endangered lists for over fifty years.

Here you see a right whale with her young
swimming right on top of its mother. The calf
should be about one-third to one-half the size
of the mother.

DOLPHINS

Bottle-nosed dolphin

Perhaps the most widely known of the whale family, the bottle-nosed dolphin is certainly the most popular.

The dolphin has been considered the friend of man since the dawn of Greek history.

In the past thirty years we have learned much new information about dolphins, including something of their complex language of sounds.

There are many species, including the killer whale—the largest of the dolphins.

We will be concerned with the killer whale and the bottle-nosed dolphin.

In captivity,
the bottle-nosed learns any
number of tricks
very quickly.
     This bottle-nosed has
learned to pull a
dinner bell in no
uncertain fashion,
while his friend
waits below.

Mother and daughter out for a tour. Young dolphins stay close to their mothers for at least twelve months. Like most mammals, dolphin mothers are extremely protective.

More than one report tells of dolphins defending themselves and their young against killer whales. This is very effectively done by swimming a full 35 knots (35 nautical miles, or 64.8 km) per hour into the side of the attacker. Dolphins have been known to drive off a killer whale and to kill an attacking shark, yet they are unfailingly gentle with humans and never lose their playfulness.

Killer whale

Orca, the killer whale, travels in packs of a half dozen or more. It is a relentless hunter in the open seas and has been known to attack older great whales. The killer whale is feared by seals, fish, other dolphins, and walruses. Yet in captivity it is gentle with humans and easily trained.

This will be your first try at putting together a group. The way you place them and their relationships to each other are very important.

Orca as a performer

Killer whales can be trained to do all the feats that dolphins do. This is astonishing, considering that, at 25 feet (7.6 m) long, they are much larger than dolphins.

SEALS

As sea lion pups have to be taught to swim and breathe in water, they must be encouraged to enter the water, something they almost never do of their own accord.

Here's mama hoping her cubs will get the message. Frequently they have to be forced.

Your challenge here, aside from the main drawing, will be to give each surface—water, rock, and seals—its own quite different texture.

Unlike the shark, whale, or dolphin,
sea lions use their front flippers to propel
themselves, and their hind ones to steer. This
makes a big difference in how you show them.

As you can see, sea lions are very flexible
while in the water, playing, pursuing a meal, or
being pursued.

Sketch the seals in pencil and two tones of
wash.

A young bull walrus is shown alone
because he has probably been chased away and
exiled for a time. When he becomes mature and
heavy enough to displace one of the older bulls,
he will reassert himself. Walruses are very gentle
and are aroused only when threatened.

Try this first in pencil and then do a wash
version.

Sea elephant

The bull sea elephant, largest of the true seal family, can weigh in at 2½ tons fully grown. They are fun to draw because of their large noses.

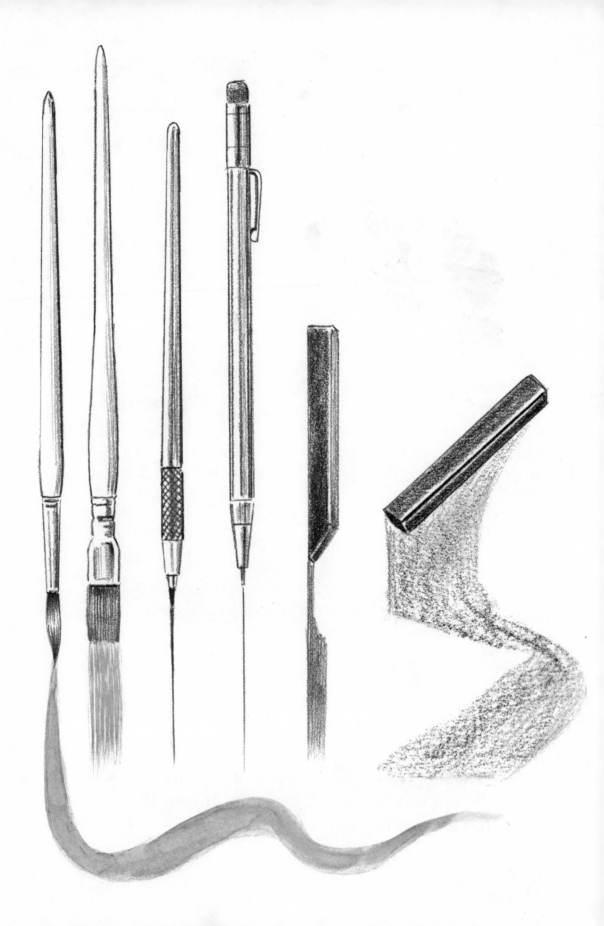

CHAPTER 6
Tools and Techniques

Improving your drawing skills should always be your first concern. High on the list of second considerations should be the use of familiar as well as new tools and techniques.

Several words of caution: You should always be able to look at a drawing and have your first thought be, "What a good drawing!" You should never have to say, "What good rendering, great technique, *and* a nice drawing too!" Never let your tools or a technique become more important than the drawing.

Now, down to a few facts, beginning with several ways to hold a pencil. Until you find something that pleases you more, continue to use HB, 2H, 2B, or 4B (according to the dampness of the weather) pencils—plain or automatic—or lead holders.

There are several ways to hold a pencil, but only two of these allow you to hold it in a relaxed way and still keep full fluid control.

First is the way most of us learn when we begin to write (A).

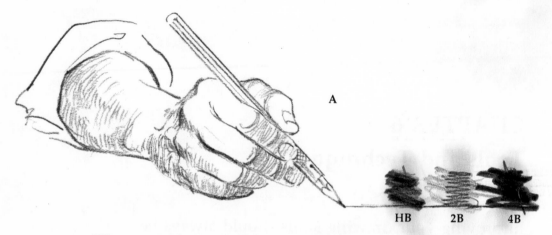

HB   2B   4B

The second way is to hold the pencil between thumb and forefinger and support it by your second finger and the underside of your palm (B). Both allow the maximum use of your wrist and specific control at the same time.

Most important of all, remember to hold the pencil, brush, or pen in a gentle way.

There are many types of pencils. However, you will probably find three kinds most useful—graphite, charcoal, and lithograph. All three also come in compressed sticks.

You can sharpen them all—including the compressed sticks—into the usual pencil point or you can make a chisel point. This can make a thin line (A-1) or a broad line (A-2), depending upon how you hold it.

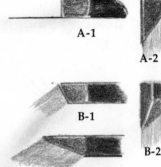

A-1

A-2

B-1

Types of chisel points

B-2

B-3

You can make the chisel point a wedge (B-1) and (B-2). The degree of wedge will determine the width of line you can make (B-3).

If the compressed sticks appeal to you, you can cover a very large area with tone by using one of the long, flat sides. You can, of course, make a very thin line by using one of the edges.

When not using the flat side, wrap the stick with facial tissue (C). It keeps you much cleaner!

C

Pen and ink is an exciting medium but not as flexible as pencil, and your mistakes are harder to change. But as your work matures, experiment with combinations: pen, ink, and wash, for example.

As with any instrument, be sure to hold the pen in a very relaxed fashion.

If you are using only pen and ink, a hard, smooth paper is needed.

In order to find the best pen nib for your work, you will have to experiment. For a start, try Gillot #290 or Hunt's finest. They are both strong and flexible enough to make both fine and broad strokes.

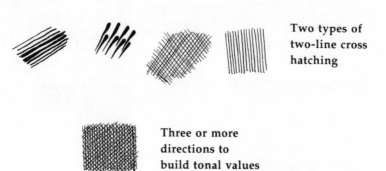

Two types of two-line cross hatching

Three or more directions to build tonal values

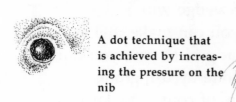

A dot technique that is achieved by increasing the pressure on the nib

This shows, in a very limited way, the use of a combination of pen, ink, and wash.

There are, of course, other uses and techniques. These you should find in your own way. Experimenting is one of the ways you'll have the most fun and get the most interesting results.

The brush is perhaps the most versatile of all tools. It also requires the most practice in order to handle it with ease.

You can make a simple line drawing with a brush. You can also use lampblack (water-soluble black paint) and water to render a black and white painting with many tones of gray.

Buy a #2 or #4 red sable brush and a tube of lampblack. *Warning:* The brush will be very expensive but the cheap ones don't last and are not a good investment.

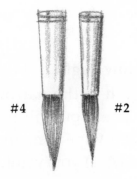

#4   #2

With practice you can make all of the strokes for pen (see page 61). When you are quite sure of yourself, you can draw with a brush. One of the two most used methods is dry brush; the other is keeping the brush quite wet.

For dry brush, use two jars of water; one to rinse your brush when you change tone, the other to dilute the small amount of lampblack you've placed on a plate.

Make a puddle of tone and dip the brush into the tone. Then, pressing gently, draw the brush across a blotter until it is fairly dry and looks flattened out, like A.

A

A-1
Dry

A-2
Wet

Now begin to build your tonal values, turning the brush to the narrow edge when you need a fine line. You will have to refill your brush and then wipe it many times to achieve the results (A-1) you want.

For darker areas you will increase the amount of lampblack you use.

For a wet rendering (A-2), you'll need watercolor paper. Make a light pencil sketch and with a sponge dampen the area to be covered with tone. Work quickly until the area begins to dry. Again dampen with the sponge and begin your work once more.

Working on wet paper is tricky. You will learn only from practice. When you've got the hang of it, you can get some wonderful "wet look" results.

Both techniques are difficult but worth the effort.

Pencil

On this and the next two pages you will see the same sketch done in four different mediums: pencil, pencil and wash, pen and ink, and wash alone.

Try them. You will learn something from each effort.

Pencil and wash

Pen and ink

Wash

SUMMARY

Unless you have a solid foundation, the end product in drawing will probably not be good. Try to remember that when you are tempted to skip all the step-by-step work that is essential—all the parts of learning that seem less than fun.

When you don't feel like drawing anymore, don't do it. Don't force yourself. Take off, do whatever pleases you; just cut loose. But save the results of what you've just done. In a week or so, go back and look at the drawings. If they are the best you've ever done, it will be most unusual, because development is not necessarily consistent. If they are not, it will help show you your weaknesses and the areas that need strengthening.

Above all, don't be discouraged. We all learn and develop at different rates. If you enjoy drawing and it holds your interest, keep working. In the end you'll have a skill that will bring you great joy and satisfaction.

The best of luck!